# KUMI NA MOJA
# NEW-GENERATION AFRICAN POETS
## A CHAPBOOK BOX SET

INTRODUCTION BY

**KWAME DAWES & CHRIS ABANI**

Published by Akashic Books


ISBN for full box set: 978-1-63614-241-8
Library of Congress Control Number for full box set: 2025935093


Printed in China
First printing

EU Authorized Representative details:
Easy Access System Europe
Mustamäe tee 50, 10621 Tallinn, Estonia
gpsr.request@easproject.com

Akashic Books
Brooklyn, New York
Instagram, X, Facebook:
AkashicBooks
info@akashicbooks.com
www.akashicbooks.com

African Poetry Book Fund
Brown University
10 Prospect Street
Box A
Providence, RI 02912
apbf@brown.edu

*For Lorna,*
*Sena, Kekeli, Akua,*
*Mama the Great,*
*and the tribe: Gwyneth, Kojo, Adjoa, and Kojovi.*
*Remembering Aba and Neville.*
*K.D.*

*

*Remembering Daphne, Michael, and Greg;*
*and for Mark, Charles, and Stella—my family.*
*I love you.*
*C.A.*

# KUMI NA MOJA: NEW-GENERATION AFRICAN POETS

*Introduction by Kwame Dawes and Chris Abani*

## CONTENTS OF BOX SET

# KUMI NA MOJA: NEW-GENERATION AFRICAN POETS

*Introduction*
*by Kwame Dawes and Chris Abani*

## Part One

One of the core features of this chapbook series has been our collaborations with African artists, whose works give power and visual meaning to the wonderful poems we publish. For years, the process has been marked by meticulous care and selectivity in finding the right artist for each box set, and the stunning serendipitous magic achieved between the artwork and each chapbook. Over the years, we have noted African artists whose works have gained attention in the media and been shown in numerous galleries in Africa and around the world. We have developed a list of artists we admire, a list that keeps growing. As the production march takes us toward the design of the box set, we start to scour websites of galleries, collections, agencies, and the personal websites and social media profiles of many of these artists, trying to think of ways artwork can translate to book covers, taking into account its variety and coherence, as well as the less definable consideration of sensibility. We also have a group of correspondents whom we ask for recommendations for artists they think would be amenable to the spirit of this project. Typically, we are seeking art for ten to thirteen chapbooks, plus the box set cover, making it necessary to ask artists for access to quite a few pieces to be featured in this virtual gallery. A short list almost always emerges, and then we do the ask. We have been incredibly fortunate to be well received by artists who immediately saw the value of this project, and who have thrown themselves into the partnership with incredible generosity and energy. It is at this point that the brilliant Aaron Petrovich begins his remarkable work of marrying works of art with individual chapbooks.

For the past two editions of our chapbook series, however, the approach has been somewhat different, not so much by design as by the inclination of our artists. Last year, Ethiopian American artist Kokeb Zeleke agreed to provide the cover art for the box set. She was aware of the series and offered to create covers based on her reading of each chapbook. We sent her the chapbooks, and she began to work. When she sent us her artwork, we knew we were dealing with something quite remarkable. Aaron made a few decisions about the pieces that would be used, but he insisted that his task was exciting rather than difficult. What I found especially striking was that when we shared the cover designs with the poets, their approval was unanimous. Without knowing, they simply assumed that the artwork was created with their poems in mind, because it captured their poetic intentions for the collection. This year, we contracted another fantastic Ethiopian artist to create covers, and she too indicated that she would like to work on the poetry collections. The box set you now have in hand features some amazing work by Mulu Legesse, a gifted artist who works on the continent and who has read the poems with sensitivity and care.

One might wonder why I would devote so much of this introduction to the art that graces the cover of the box set. The reason is simple: I want to make clear just how much care goes into this project, which is deeply rooted in the idea of an artistic force that we see happening throughout Africa. We are also trying to engender greater collaborative acts like this one. The African Poetry Book Fund has a policy that all our cover art will feature the work of African artists, and we make every effort to ensure that the entire production process is an organic expression of African artistry.

This year, we feature ten emerging African poets. It bears observing that six of the ten poets in this box set are Nigerians. Given that the selection process is largely a blind one, it is striking that Nigerian poets are so heavily featured. Of course, there are reasons of demographics, language, and tradition that may explain some of this. Yet one would be hard-pressed not to see in these poems the rich diversity of Nigerian culture and art. The poets come from quite different backgrounds—some from journalism, some from the cultural milieu of a Yoruba Muslim. Further, the power of human expression in their work reminds us that we are dealing with a cadre of poets who are teaching us a great deal about the Africa of today. We are excited to have included, along with those from Nigeria, a cluster of poets from regions less frequently represented in our publishing enterprise, including Namibia, Liberia, and Botswana. This collection of chapbooks stands out greatly for its stylistic variation. At times, the matter may be one of form, and at other times, one of language. In some instances, what we observe are the ways in which spirituality is explored, or how the landscape is engaged. This variety assures us that the poets are pressing forward to find their own distinctive voices and to respond to their worlds with care and inquisitiveness.

It is often easy to forget how much has changed in African poetry in the last decade and a half. In the early part of the twenty-first century, Chris Abani and I were thinking a great deal about the position of African poetry in the world and in Africa. We observed that, without books by African poets in broad circulation, there would be the impression that Africans were not writing poetry, and the presumption that there were no poetic traditions in Africa, nor was there a modern African poetic force that would bring a great deal to our understanding of global and African cultures. The APBF was conceived with the specific goal of flooding the world with books by African poets, so as to create a certain kind of knowledge base for other publishers and editors to start paying attention to the poetry being produced in Africa. We have never perceived ourselves as conventional publishers, but as instigators and activists in the publishing world. Clearly, we have become, for good reason, more than instigators of publishing African poetry. In the APBF and especially in this chapbook series, we have, by design, created an entity that is fully aware that publishing alone is not enough. We also know that African poetry did not begin in the twenty-first century, and that, without creating access to the long history of African poetry for our contemporary writers, we will stifle their creative possibilities. Even as we have created mechanisms for research into the history of African poetry, and into an accounting of African poetry in all its forms, we also feel deeply engaged by projects like this one, which give a taste of contemporary African poetry.

In the end, one remains appreciative of the coherence of vision and intention that makes such a beautiful publication like this possible. Our poets are the products of the artistic forces of their cultures and their lived existences in Africa and its diaspora. We are constantly being gifted with dispatches from the "windows" of African people: gifts offered in lines of poetry, in images, in rhymes and rhythms, and packaged in caring design, editing, and copyediting—an artistic collaboration that seeks, at its core, to derive its meaning and power from the aesthetic multivalence of African life and culture.

*Kwame Dawes*

## Part Two

We have been doing this for ten years now. Long enough that it should be easy, or at least easier, with every approach, every iteration. That would make sense if these introductions were mere rote, an academic exercise. It would be easy to continue from where the conversation left off. But this journey has always involved a good amount of careful preparation, a whole lot of community support, and an inordinate amount of luck. Over the years, a lot of thinking has gone into the shape of this project—not just the chapbook collection, but also the first book prize, the editing and republishing and repositioning of mid-career and elder poets from the continent, libraries, educational possibilities, partnerships, and, of course, the ever-haunting future.

The humbling thing about cocurating a project like this is that you are always adapting to things beyond your control. The best laid plans, while required, and built on a lot of skill and education, are nothing compared to the courage it takes to establish this ground, and to try to grow a hope that fits into the gaps of a vast and ancient lineage of letters. If all works out, you will never see how far forward into the future it reaches.

What is not often talked about regarding hope and courage is that these are journeys you cannot travel alone. There is the biological lineage that supports and girdles you from both sides of the divide. There is the joy and sacrifice and unquestioning support of your immediate family—the dreams they sometimes set aside for you to have yours. The writers, young and old, who trust us with their work, with helping them shape a music that will sustain a career for them for years to come. The way these writers come to believe in and give themselves wholeheartedly to the vision of a quilted future of letters. The friends you have been gifted with—other poets, writers, and even publishers, who, when you call upon their help, say, of course, whatever you need. And you will call on them, again and again, and they will say yes, again and again. At considerable cost to their time and their own projects, and with no compensation beyond your eternal gratitude and an investment in a future of poetry and poets that will, if this goes well, eclipse them, eclipse us all. This invigorates rather than scares our editorial team and our gallant publishing partners, Akashic Books and the University of Nebraska Press. Still, you think, we are engaged in a call to duty that will make all these gifts, all these sacrifices, worthwhile. But you never really know. You hope.

That you stand with a brother back-to-back is something you both lean on with the surety of blood. Your successes and losses are intertwined in ways you could never have foreseen. But what you are never prepared for are the strangers who step into the ring of fire, often unsolicited, and who offer themselves to this hope you carry. Many of them are closeted and private poets whose lives and duties have taken them down other paths; some of them have no connection to the continent other than a rumor of this vision you share; how it connects to some hope in them, you may never know. Where am I going with these words, you may ask? Well, I am Igbo in culture, worldview, and DNA—garrulous, but also pointed.

So much about African letters is a struggle with inscription and erasure. Many old African cultures, from Egypt to Ethiopia, Southern Africa to the West Coast, had a written language. With the interruption and devastation of trade and colonial occupations, and the targeting of indigenous nobility, much of the knowledge around these scripts vanished. At the time of European contact, certain linguistic and written modes of language were limited to the use of elite groups. As Europe expanded, so did the need for educated non-elites to help run colonies. Script and language became more accessible for Europeans, but Africans suffered the opposite. This has meant that written modes, even in indigenous continental languages, have followed European influence. The struggle to articulate the self within the confines of these new language modes has often led to conflict between modernist, nationalist, and recovered selves. A new elite seeks to distance themselves from a past they feel embarrassed by, while younger generations pursue recuperation, restoration, and the inevitable negotiations with sentimentality and the romantic. Though these negotiations have moved from the establishment of authentic political selves, we still see them even in these very recent books.

In newer work, we see a shift from the establishment of a "true" African identity, one opposed to Western definitions, to more inward conversations where the concerns are no longer between poets and the West, but between poets and their own cultures. Patriarchy and its claims to the definition and circumscription of women in Africa, gender as an entire field, and the arenas of sexuality and difference are the new terrains of engagement. While these are political struggles, they have become more complicated, ignoring the history of colonialism and negotiating more directly with African cultures and selves in a way that bypasses the sentimental and romantic leanings of previous generations and instead homes in on a more robust engagement. This is not a critique of the writing lineage we all descend from, because writers did their best to lay what became the liberating terrain that makes the rest of us possible. And it is also not to say that, even early on, there weren't writers who were kin to these newer ones (Soyinka and his stand vis-à-vis Negritude, for example, or Cyprian Ekwensi, whose project had a capaciousness that Achebe lacked). But there is a marked turn that the poets in these chapbooks (both this collection and prior box sets) have shown the scholarship around these new letters to be either entirely absent or lacking the capaciousness in approach. With much of the critical framework still focused on postcolonial and transnational positions, it is increasingly clear that the creative output has outgrown it.

This shift may be because the writers are mostly from groups that didn't have access to publication in large numbers, including women and queer-leaning writers. Or maybe not. Hence my invitation for updated critical frameworks from scholars working in this field who are not focused on prose.

In the collection *A Body in Spice*, Roseline Mgbodichinma engages with erasure and inscription using items that straddle domesticity and trade. She examines how masculinities have tried to usurp the discovery of items that, like salt, have become precious and important. This engagement covers everything from how the tyranny of the state gets reflected in the tyranny of the family, to war (and the erasure of women from war), to marriage. We see imported forms like the ghazal, as well as experimental breaking of syntax.

In *Ashes*, Rahma Jimoh invokes both these ideas in the opening lines of the very first poem, "Playacting":

> water holds you in its long hands.
> and the lines on your palms open pathways for you.

All the way through this collection, the reckoning is with the struggle between love, duty, and hope, with the inevitability of human failure measured against the effects of time. A hard-won grace is the outcome.

"The night spreads over the expansive savanna like soot on leaves after a bushfire" is the opening line of *Bantustan Blues*. In this collection by Tjizembua Tjikuzu, as in many of the chapbooks, we begin in the devastation, in the inheritance of loss, and with only language to craft a redemptive practice.

*Humans for Sale* by Aria Deemie takes on an ever-growing problem worldwide: the trafficking of children. Trafficked children are a problem in both Africa and the Western world, and are often erased from thought because of how disruptive the idea of them has proven. The scope of the chapbook includes adults trafficked for economic reasons as well. The collection ends with a portent of hope.

Timi Sanni, in *The Ordinary Affair of Being Human*, begins the poem "Wormhole" with the line, "This is the season where grace is most difficult." My focus on first lines is partly to show how clearly each collection announces its terms, but also to show how strong the work is. Betrayal, familial and societal, are at the core of the negotiation here. A callousness, it seems, but one that is troubled by a clear vision of what causes it. The lines are lucid and razor-sharp. In "Origin Story," we read, "The blade is a dangerous thing. I killed once." If there is an antidote to the betrayals in this chapbook, it is love. Unsentimental and embodied. A rich collection.

Abdulkareem Abdulkareem's *Loss Is a Door* follows these themes. In the poem "Black River," with its allusions to slavery and the Black River in Jamaica, we see an address to the oil companies causing pollution in the Delta region of Nigeria. The idea of displacement from home, from self, is examined through the lens of a mother. And the lament is:

> . . . Even the dead
>
> are still searching for a home in the land
> ravaged by water & black oil.

The poem right after is a song of hope and possibility via the intimacy of faith, but here faith is a surrender, not in submission, but in resistance. In this chapbook, the activism employed by the art is not easy, but hard-won via intimacy and more.

In *Mouthful of Cinders*, Adesiyan Oluwapelumi comes out of the gate swinging:

> In the name of genocide,
> a father is gifted the ashes
> of his burnt daughter in an urn.

Powerful and unflinching, the measure is still the intimacy of a father's grief. This is a subtle but impactful move, one that pulls the reader into the private space of larger conflicts. People who are normally erased are the center of the narrative. We see this continued in "For Lost Boys at Sea":

> For every lost boy at sea, the tide surfs memories of lost love.
> Even the loneliness in our mute mouths creeps like a dead
> branch.

The radical centering of intimacy and love in this, and in the other chapbooks, is remarkable.

Melancholy, which is not pure sadness, but more a bittersweet yearning, drips from the lines of Michael Imossan's *The Smell of Absence*. In "What it means to be a bastard," he says:

What if I told you I
slept in my mother's skin
just to know what loneliness feels like?

Again, the negotiation is domestic and familial. The territory of loss and recuperation is wearing all the costumes of patriarchy and misguided masculinity. The poem is intimate and yet, of course, invariably national. The voice is balanced, even-tempered, with an understanding of these losses as at once personal, and the consequence of larger phenomenological movements. In "No light at the end of this story, only a question," Imossan writes:

A man leaves his unborn child
and runs toward the dark.

What is pain here is also tenderness.

Hauwa Saleh Abubakar's *Undone* is a plea for forgiveness, an attempt to reconcile with love not always being enough, and yet still reaching for it. In "Forgive Me Father, for I Have Sinned," the poem begins:

Cancer had been at the edge of my tongue
ever since I came
undone in my cousin's bathroom.

In this collection, grief is worn like a skin even as the poet attempts to flee. We get the sense that death could have been mitigated if there was money and a viable health care system. Again, the private transactions between the living, dead, and almost dead hint to larger forces. What marks these collections, and the ones preceding them, has been the turning away from the public soapbox of an earlier generation full of satire, disdain, and a certain self-importance, toward a more intimate, self-reflective space. As Abubakar says in "How to Rest a Grieving Body":

To comfort a grieving body, you must
rest it gently against another grieving body
and let them sway to the beat of memories.

And this fittingly brings me to a grief here at the APBF that is at once private and public, at once owned by members of the editorial board and yet also smudging the entire enterprise with a gentle perfume.

Our support team has been chasing me for weeks for this introduction and I have been unable to write it. Partly because, as I look again at this fine set of poets assembled here from all over the map of Africa, I am moved at what a small hope can birth. I am moved because all my skill and hard work in curating has once again failed to predict how varied these books are—aesthetically and in approach and content.

As a Babalawo, I've come to understand that when I have certain blocks, there is something at the heart of it. Yesterday, my brother Kwame informed the editorial board of the passing of one of those strangers who not only embraced the vision of the APBF, but single-handedly gave us her full support—advice (artistic, personal, and professional), financial (the lift and soaring of this ungainly bird was almost solely by her benefaction), and her friendship. But most importantly, because it is rare in the world of benefactors, she always stood back so that the Africans, the talent and visionaries and tireless workers, should steer the ship. She never took ownership or made any claim to the success she enabled to happen. A woman who carried her commitments, beliefs, and ethics with a hard-won grace. A stranger who became one more valued partner in the beating heart of this work. For the respect, friendship, and kindness she showed to the work, and, most importantly, to my brother Kwame, I dedicate this edition to you, Laura Sillerman. Travel well and visit with your extended African family of ancestors.

*Chris Abani*

**KWAME DAWES** is the author of numerous books of poetry and other works of fiction, criticism, and essays. His most recent poetry collection, *Sturge Town*, was published by Peepal Tree Press in the UK and W. W. Norton in the US. Dawes is a professor of Literary Arts at Brown University. He also teaches in the Pacific MFA Program and is the series editor of the African Poetry Book Series, director of the African Poetry Book Fund, and artistic director of the Calabash International Literary Festival. He is a Chancellor for the Academy of American Poets and a Fellow of the Royal Society of Literature. Dawes is the winner of the prestigious Windham-Campbell Prize for Poetry and was a finalist for the 2022 Neustadt International Prize for Literature. In 2022, Kwame Dawes was awarded the Order of Distinction Commander Class by the Government of Jamaica, and in 2024, he was appointed Poet Laureate of Jamaica.

**CHRIS ABANI**'s prose includes *The Secret History of Las Vegas*, *Song for Night*, *The Virgin of Flames*, *Becoming Abigail*, *GraceLand*, and *Masters of the Board*. His poetry collections include *Smoking the Bible*, *Sanctificum*, *There Are No Names for Red*, *Feed Me the Sun*, *Hands Washing Water*, *Dog Woman*, *Daphne's Lot*, and *Kalakuta Republic*. He holds a BA and MA in English, an MA in gender and culture, and a PhD in literature and creative writing. Abani is the recipient of a PEN America Freedom to Write Award, a Prince Claus Award, a Lannan Literary fellowship, a California Book Award, a Hurston/Wright Legacy Award, a PEN Beyond Margins Award, a PEN/Hemingway Award, and a Guggenheim fellowship. He won the prestigious 2024 UNT Rilke Prize and was a finalist for the 2024 Neustadt International Prize for Literature. He is also a member of the American Academy of Arts and Sciences. Born in Nigeria, he is currently on the board of trustees, a professor of English, and director of African Studies at Northwestern University.

**Mulu Legesse** was born in Addis Ababa, Ethiopia, where she grew up in a large and lively family. Her childhood was filled with adventurous experiences alongside her siblings and friends. In 2016, she pursued her dream by enrolling at the Alle School of Fine Arts and Design at Addis Ababa University, graduating with a degree in sculpture on July 1, 2019. In addition to her professional achievements, Legesse is a proud mother of one daughter. Balancing her roles as an artist and mother, she finds inspiration in both her work and family life. Legesse's work has appeared at the Addis Ababa Museum, the Moa Anbessa Art Studio Gallery, Studio 11, Post Gallery, the National Museum of Unification at Alba Iulia in Romania, Aurora Gallery, the National Museum of Egyptian Civilization, and elsewhere. Legesse's work is characterized by a deep connection to her roots and a profound exploration of cultural themes. Her exhibitions and contributions to the art world continue to inspire and resonate with audiences globally.